SHIT

I CAN'T

REMEMBER

Hello!

THIS PASSWORD

ORGANIZER IS VERY

IMPORTANT TO ME,

SO...

IF FOUND

Please
RETURN TO

_____

_____

PASSWORD
keeper

NAME :

PHONE :

EMAIL ADDRESS :

ADDRESS :

EMERGENCY CONTACTS :

Important Dates to Remember

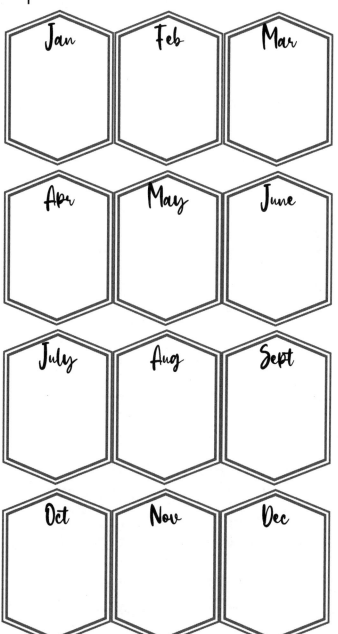

Social Media
Password Tracker

EMAIL	
USERNAME	
PASSWORD	

EMAIL	
USERNAME	
PASSWORD	

EMAIL	
USERNAME	
PASSWORD	

EMAIL	
USERNAME	
PASSWORD	

EMAIL	
USERNAME	
PASSWORD	

EMAIL	
USERNAME	
PASSWORD	

WTF is My Password?

WEBSITE
_____

USERNAME
_____

PASSWORD
_____

SECURITY QUESTIONS
_____

NOTES

WEBSITE
_____

USERNAME
_____

PASSWORD
_____

SECURITY QUESTIONS
_____

NOTES

WEBSITE
_____

USERNAME
_____

PASSWORD
_____

SECURITY QUESTIONS
_____

NOTES

WEBSITE
_____

USERNAME
_____

PASSWORD
_____

SECURITY QUESTIONS
_____

NOTES

WTF is My Password?   A

WEBSITE
_____

USERNAME
_____

PASSWORD
_____

SECURITY QUESTIONS
_____

NOTES

WEBSITE
_____

USERNAME
_____

PASSWORD
_____

SECURITY QUESTIONS
_____

NOTES

WEBSITE
_____

USERNAME
_____

PASSWORD
_____

SECURITY QUESTIONS
_____

NOTES

WEBSITE
_____

USERNAME
_____

PASSWORD
_____

SECURITY QUESTIONS
_____

NOTES

WTF is My Password?

WEBSITE

USERNAME

PASSWORD

SECURITY QUESTIONS

NOTES

WEBSITE

USERNAME

PASSWORD

SECURITY QUESTIONS

NOTES

WEBSITE

USERNAME

PASSWORD

SECURITY QUESTIONS

NOTES

WEBSITE

USERNAME

PASSWORD

SECURITY QUESTIONS

NOTES

🔒 WTF is My Password? 🔓 B

WEBSITE
_____

USERNAME
_____

PASSWORD
_____

SECURITY QUESTIONS
_____

NOTES

WEBSITE
_____

USERNAME
_____

PASSWORD
_____

SECURITY QUESTIONS
_____

NOTES

WEBSITE
_____

USERNAME
_____

PASSWORD
_____

SECURITY QUESTIONS
_____

NOTES

WEBSITE
_____

USERNAME
_____

PASSWORD
_____

SECURITY QUESTIONS
_____

NOTES

WTF is My Password?

WEBSITE
USERNAME
PASSWORD
SECURITY QUESTIONS

NOTES

WEBSITE
USERNAME
PASSWORD
SECURITY QUESTIONS

NOTES

WEBSITE
USERNAME
PASSWORD
SECURITY QUESTIONS

NOTES

WEBSITE
USERNAME
PASSWORD
SECURITY QUESTIONS

NOTES

WTF is My Password?

WEBSITE

USERNAME

PASSWORD

SECURITY QUESTIONS

NOTES

WEBSITE

USERNAME

PASSWORD

SECURITY QUESTIONS

NOTES

WEBSITE

USERNAME

PASSWORD

SECURITY QUESTIONS

NOTES

WEBSITE

USERNAME

PASSWORD

SECURITY QUESTIONS

NOTES

WTF is My Password?

WEBSITE
_____

USERNAME
_____

PASSWORD
_____

SECURITY QUESTIONS
_____

NOTES

WEBSITE
_____

USERNAME
_____

PASSWORD
_____

SECURITY QUESTIONS
_____

NOTES

WEBSITE
_____

USERNAME
_____

PASSWORD
_____

SECURITY QUESTIONS
_____

NOTES

WEBSITE
_____

USERNAME
_____

PASSWORD
_____

SECURITY QUESTIONS
_____

NOTES

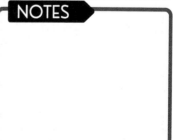

WTF is My Password? C

WEBSITE

USERNAME

PASSWORD

SECURITY QUESTIONS

NOTES

WEBSITE

USERNAME

PASSWORD

SECURITY QUESTIONS

NOTES

WEBSITE

USERNAME

PASSWORD

SECURITY QUESTIONS

NOTES

WEBSITE

USERNAME

PASSWORD

SECURITY QUESTIONS

NOTES

WTF is My Password?

WEBSITE

USERNAME

PASSWORD

SECURITY QUESTIONS

NOTES

WEBSITE

USERNAME

PASSWORD

SECURITY QUESTIONS

NOTES

WEBSITE

USERNAME

PASSWORD

SECURITY QUESTIONS

NOTES

WEBSITE

USERNAME

PASSWORD

SECURITY QUESTIONS

NOTES

WTF is My Password? D

WEBSITE

_____

USERNAME

_____

PASSWORD

_____

SECURITY QUESTIONS

_____

WEBSITE

_____

USERNAME

_____

PASSWORD

_____

SECURITY QUESTIONS

_____

WEBSITE

_____

USERNAME

_____

PASSWORD

_____

SECURITY QUESTIONS

_____

WEBSITE

_____

USERNAME

_____

PASSWORD

_____

SECURITY QUESTIONS

_____

🔒 WTF is My Password? 🔒 D

WEBSITE
_____
USERNAME
_____
PASSWORD
_____
SECURITY QUESTIONS
_____

NOTES

WEBSITE
_____
USERNAME
_____
PASSWORD
_____
SECURITY QUESTIONS
_____

NOTES

WEBSITE
_____
USERNAME
_____
PASSWORD
_____
SECURITY QUESTIONS
_____

NOTES

WEBSITE
_____
USERNAME
_____
PASSWORD
_____
SECURITY QUESTIONS
_____

NOTES

WTF is My Password? D

WEBSITE
_____

USERNAME
_____

PASSWORD
_____

SECURITY QUESTIONS
_____

NOTES

WEBSITE
_____

USERNAME
_____

PASSWORD
_____

SECURITY QUESTIONS
_____

NOTES

WEBSITE
_____

USERNAME
_____

PASSWORD
_____

SECURITY QUESTIONS
_____

NOTES

WEBSITE
_____

USERNAME
_____

PASSWORD
_____

SECURITY QUESTIONS
_____

NOTES

🔒 WTF is My Password? 🔒 E

WEBSITE
_____

USERNAME
_____

PASSWORD
_____

SECURITY QUESTIONS
_____

NOTES

WEBSITE
_____

USERNAME
_____

PASSWORD
_____

SECURITY QUESTIONS
_____

NOTES

WEBSITE
_____

USERNAME
_____

PASSWORD
_____

SECURITY QUESTIONS
_____

NOTES

WEBSITE
_____

USERNAME
_____

PASSWORD
_____

SECURITY QUESTIONS
_____

NOTES

WTF is My Password? E

WEBSITE

USERNAME

PASSWORD

SECURITY QUESTIONS

NOTES

WEBSITE

USERNAME

PASSWORD

SECURITY QUESTIONS

NOTES

WEBSITE

USERNAME

PASSWORD

SECURITY QUESTIONS

NOTES

WEBSITE

USERNAME

PASSWORD

SECURITY QUESTIONS

NOTES

WTF is My Password?

WEBSITE
_____
USERNAME
_____
PASSWORD
_____
SECURITY QUESTIONS
_____

NOTES

WEBSITE
_____
USERNAME
_____
PASSWORD
_____
SECURITY QUESTIONS
_____

NOTES

WEBSITE
_____
USERNAME
_____
PASSWORD
_____
SECURITY QUESTIONS
_____

NOTES

WEBSITE
_____
USERNAME
_____
PASSWORD
_____
SECURITY QUESTIONS
_____

NOTES

WTF is My Password? F

WEBSITE
_____
USERNAME
_____
PASSWORD
_____
SECURITY QUESTIONS
_____

NOTES

WEBSITE
_____
USERNAME
_____
PASSWORD
_____
SECURITY QUESTIONS
_____

NOTES

WEBSITE
_____
USERNAME
_____
PASSWORD
_____
SECURITY QUESTIONS
_____

NOTES

WEBSITE
_____
USERNAME
_____
PASSWORD
_____
SECURITY QUESTIONS
_____

NOTES

🔒 WTF is My Password? 🔓 F

WEBSITE
_____

USERNAME
_____

PASSWORD
_____

SECURITY QUESTIONS
_____

NOTES

WEBSITE
_____

USERNAME
_____

PASSWORD
_____

SECURITY QUESTIONS
_____

NOTES

WEBSITE
_____

USERNAME
_____

PASSWORD
_____

SECURITY QUESTIONS
_____

NOTES

WEBSITE
_____

USERNAME
_____

PASSWORD
_____

SECURITY QUESTIONS
_____

NOTES

WTF is My Password? F

WEBSITE
_____

USERNAME
_____

PASSWORD
_____

SECURITY QUESTIONS
_____

NOTES

WEBSITE
_____

USERNAME
_____

PASSWORD
_____

SECURITY QUESTIONS
_____

NOTES

WEBSITE
_____

USERNAME
_____

PASSWORD
_____

SECURITY QUESTIONS
_____

NOTES

WEBSITE
_____

USERNAME
_____

PASSWORD
_____

SECURITY QUESTIONS
_____

NOTES

WTF is My Password?

WEBSITE

USERNAME

PASSWORD

SECURITY QUESTIONS

NOTES

WEBSITE

USERNAME

PASSWORD

SECURITY QUESTIONS

NOTES

WEBSITE

USERNAME

PASSWORD

SECURITY QUESTIONS

NOTES

WEBSITE

USERNAME

PASSWORD

SECURITY QUESTIONS

NOTES

🔒 WTF is My Password? 🔒 [G]

WEBSITE
_____

USERNAME
_____

PASSWORD
_____

SECURITY QUESTIONS
_____

NOTES

WEBSITE
_____

USERNAME
_____

PASSWORD
_____

SECURITY QUESTIONS
_____

NOTES

WEBSITE
_____

USERNAME
_____

PASSWORD
_____

SECURITY QUESTIONS
_____

NOTES

WEBSITE
_____

USERNAME
_____

PASSWORD
_____

SECURITY QUESTIONS
_____

NOTES

 WTF is My Password?

WEBSITE

_____

USERNAME

_____

PASSWORD

_____

SECURITY QUESTIONS

_____

NOTES

WEBSITE

_____

USERNAME

_____

PASSWORD

_____

SECURITY QUESTIONS

_____

NOTES

WEBSITE

_____

USERNAME

_____

PASSWORD

_____

SECURITY QUESTIONS

_____

NOTES

WEBSITE

_____

USERNAME

_____

PASSWORD

_____

SECURITY QUESTIONS

_____

NOTES

WTF is My Password?

H

WEBSITE

USERNAME

PASSWORD

SECURITY QUESTIONS

NOTES

WEBSITE

USERNAME

PASSWORD

SECURITY QUESTIONS

NOTES

WEBSITE

USERNAME

PASSWORD

SECURITY QUESTIONS

NOTES

WEBSITE

USERNAME

PASSWORD

SECURITY QUESTIONS

NOTES

 WTF is My Password?

WEBSITE

_____

USERNAME

_____

PASSWORD

_____

SECURITY QUESTIONS

_____

NOTES

WEBSITE

_____

USERNAME

_____

PASSWORD

_____

SECURITY QUESTIONS

_____

NOTES

WEBSITE

_____

USERNAME

_____

PASSWORD

_____

SECURITY QUESTIONS

_____

NOTES

WEBSITE

_____

USERNAME

_____

PASSWORD

_____

SECURITY QUESTIONS

_____

NOTES

🔒 WTF is My Password? 🔒

WEBSITE

_____

USERNAME

_____

PASSWORD

_____

SECURITY QUESTIONS

_____

NOTES

WEBSITE

_____

USERNAME

_____

PASSWORD

_____

SECURITY QUESTIONS

_____

NOTES

WEBSITE

_____

USERNAME

_____

PASSWORD

_____

SECURITY QUESTIONS

_____

NOTES

WEBSITE

_____

USERNAME

_____

PASSWORD

_____

SECURITY QUESTIONS

_____

NOTES

WTF is My Password?

WEBSITE

USERNAME

PASSWORD

SECURITY QUESTIONS

NOTES

WEBSITE

USERNAME

PASSWORD

SECURITY QUESTIONS

NOTES

WEBSITE

USERNAME

PASSWORD

SECURITY QUESTIONS

NOTES

WEBSITE

USERNAME

PASSWORD

SECURITY QUESTIONS

NOTES

🔒 WTF is My Password? 🔒 | 1 |

WEBSITE
_____

USERNAME
_____

PASSWORD
_____

SECURITY QUESTIONS
_____

WEBSITE
_____

USERNAME
_____

PASSWORD
_____

SECURITY QUESTIONS
_____

WEBSITE
_____

USERNAME
_____

PASSWORD
_____

SECURITY QUESTIONS
_____

WEBSITE
_____

USERNAME
_____

PASSWORD
_____

SECURITY QUESTIONS
_____

 # WTF is My Password?

WEBSITE
_____

USERNAME
_____

PASSWORD
_____

SECURITY QUESTIONS
_____

NOTES

WEBSITE
_____

USERNAME
_____

PASSWORD
_____

SECURITY QUESTIONS
_____

NOTES

WEBSITE
_____

USERNAME
_____

PASSWORD
_____

SECURITY QUESTIONS
_____

NOTES

WEBSITE
_____

USERNAME
_____

PASSWORD
_____

SECURITY QUESTIONS
_____

NOTES

🔒 WTF is My Password? 🔒

WEBSITE
_____

USERNAME
_____

PASSWORD
_____

SECURITY QUESTIONS
_____

NOTES

WEBSITE
_____

USERNAME
_____

PASSWORD
_____

SECURITY QUESTIONS
_____

NOTES

WEBSITE
_____

USERNAME
_____

PASSWORD
_____

SECURITY QUESTIONS
_____

NOTES

WEBSITE
_____

USERNAME
_____

PASSWORD
_____

SECURITY QUESTIONS
_____

NOTES

WTF is My Password?

WEBSITE

USERNAME

PASSWORD

SECURITY QUESTIONS

NOTES

WEBSITE

USERNAME

PASSWORD

SECURITY QUESTIONS

NOTES

WEBSITE

USERNAME

PASSWORD

SECURITY QUESTIONS

NOTES

WEBSITE

USERNAME

PASSWORD

SECURITY QUESTIONS

NOTES

WTF is My Password?

WEBSITE

_____

USERNAME

_____

PASSWORD

_____

SECURITY QUESTIONS

_____

NOTES

WEBSITE

_____

USERNAME

_____

PASSWORD

_____

SECURITY QUESTIONS

_____

NOTES

WEBSITE

_____

USERNAME

_____

PASSWORD

_____

SECURITY QUESTIONS

_____

NOTES

WEBSITE

_____

USERNAME

_____

PASSWORD

_____

SECURITY QUESTIONS

_____

NOTES

 # WTF is My Password?

K

WEBSITE
_____

USERNAME
_____

PASSWORD
_____

SECURITY QUESTIONS
_____

NOTES

WEBSITE
_____

USERNAME
_____

PASSWORD
_____

SECURITY QUESTIONS
_____

NOTES

WEBSITE
_____

USERNAME
_____

PASSWORD
_____

SECURITY QUESTIONS
_____

NOTES

WEBSITE
_____

USERNAME
_____

PASSWORD
_____

SECURITY QUESTIONS
_____

NOTES

WTF is My Password?

WEBSITE

_____

USERNAME

_____

PASSWORD

_____

SECURITY QUESTIONS

_____

NOTES

WEBSITE

_____

USERNAME

_____

PASSWORD

_____

SECURITY QUESTIONS

_____

NOTES

WEBSITE

_____

USERNAME

_____

PASSWORD

_____

SECURITY QUESTIONS

_____

NOTES

WEBSITE

_____

USERNAME

_____

PASSWORD

_____

SECURITY QUESTIONS

_____

NOTES

 WTF is My Password?

WEBSITE
_____

USERNAME
_____

PASSWORD
_____

SECURITY QUESTIONS
_____

NOTES

WEBSITE
_____

USERNAME
_____

PASSWORD
_____

SECURITY QUESTIONS
_____

NOTES

WEBSITE
_____

USERNAME
_____

PASSWORD
_____

SECURITY QUESTIONS
_____

NOTES

WEBSITE
_____

USERNAME
_____

PASSWORD
_____

SECURITY QUESTIONS
_____

NOTES

🔒 WTF is My Password? 🔒 L

WEBSITE
_____

USERNAME
_____

PASSWORD
_____

SECURITY QUESTIONS
_____

NOTES

WEBSITE
_____

USERNAME
_____

PASSWORD
_____

SECURITY QUESTIONS
_____

NOTES

WEBSITE
_____

USERNAME
_____

PASSWORD
_____

SECURITY QUESTIONS
_____

NOTES

WEBSITE
_____

USERNAME
_____

PASSWORD
_____

SECURITY QUESTIONS
_____

NOTES

WTF is My Password? L

WEBSITE

USERNAME

PASSWORD

SECURITY QUESTIONS

NOTES

WEBSITE

USERNAME

PASSWORD

SECURITY QUESTIONS

NOTES

WEBSITE

USERNAME

PASSWORD

SECURITY QUESTIONS

NOTES

WEBSITE

USERNAME

PASSWORD

SECURITY QUESTIONS

NOTES

WTF is My Password? L

WEBSITE
_____

USERNAME
_____

PASSWORD
_____

SECURITY QUESTIONS
_____

NOTES

WEBSITE
_____

USERNAME
_____

PASSWORD
_____

SECURITY QUESTIONS
_____

NOTES

WEBSITE
_____

USERNAME
_____

PASSWORD
_____

SECURITY QUESTIONS
_____

NOTES

WEBSITE
_____

USERNAME
_____

PASSWORD
_____

SECURITY QUESTIONS
_____

NOTES

 # WTF is My Password?

WEBSITE
_____
USERNAME
_____
PASSWORD
_____
SECURITY QUESTIONS
_____

NOTES

WEBSITE
_____
USERNAME
_____
PASSWORD
_____
SECURITY QUESTIONS
_____

NOTES

WEBSITE
_____
USERNAME
_____
PASSWORD
_____
SECURITY QUESTIONS
_____

NOTES

WEBSITE
_____
USERNAME
_____
PASSWORD
_____
SECURITY QUESTIONS
_____

NOTES

WTF is My Password?

WEBSITE

USERNAME

PASSWORD

SECURITY QUESTIONS

NOTES

WEBSITE

USERNAME

PASSWORD

SECURITY QUESTIONS

NOTES

WEBSITE

USERNAME

PASSWORD

SECURITY QUESTIONS

NOTES

WEBSITE

USERNAME

PASSWORD

SECURITY QUESTIONS

NOTES

 WTF is My Password?

WEBSITE
_____

USERNAME
_____

PASSWORD
_____

SECURITY QUESTIONS
_____

NOTES

WEBSITE
_____

USERNAME
_____

PASSWORD
_____

SECURITY QUESTIONS
_____

NOTES

WEBSITE
_____

USERNAME
_____

PASSWORD
_____

SECURITY QUESTIONS
_____

NOTES

WEBSITE
_____

USERNAME
_____

PASSWORD
_____

SECURITY QUESTIONS
_____

NOTES

🔒 WTF is My Password? 🔓 N

WEBSITE
_____

USERNAME
_____

PASSWORD
_____

SECURITY QUESTIONS
_____

NOTES

WEBSITE
_____

USERNAME
_____

PASSWORD
_____

SECURITY QUESTIONS
_____

NOTES

WEBSITE
_____

USERNAME
_____

PASSWORD
_____

SECURITY QUESTIONS
_____

NOTES

WEBSITE
_____

USERNAME
_____

PASSWORD
_____

SECURITY QUESTIONS
_____

NOTES

WTF is My Password?

WEBSITE

USERNAME

PASSWORD

SECURITY QUESTIONS

NOTES

WEBSITE

USERNAME

PASSWORD

SECURITY QUESTIONS

NOTES

WEBSITE

USERNAME

PASSWORD

SECURITY QUESTIONS

NOTES

WEBSITE

USERNAME

PASSWORD

SECURITY QUESTIONS

NOTES

 # WTF is My Password?

WEBSITE

_____

USERNAME

_____

PASSWORD

_____

SECURITY QUESTIONS

_____

NOTES

WEBSITE

_____

USERNAME

_____

PASSWORD

_____

SECURITY QUESTIONS

_____

NOTES

WEBSITE

_____

USERNAME

_____

PASSWORD

_____

SECURITY QUESTIONS

_____

NOTES

WEBSITE

_____

USERNAME

_____

PASSWORD

_____

SECURITY QUESTIONS

_____

NOTES

WTF is My Password?

WEBSITE

_____

USERNAME

_____

PASSWORD

_____

SECURITY QUESTIONS

_____

NOTES

WEBSITE

_____

USERNAME

_____

PASSWORD

_____

SECURITY QUESTIONS

_____

NOTES

WEBSITE

_____

USERNAME

_____

PASSWORD

_____

SECURITY QUESTIONS

_____

NOTES

WEBSITE

_____

USERNAME

_____

PASSWORD

_____

SECURITY QUESTIONS

_____

NOTES

WTF is My Password?

WEBSITE

_____

USERNAME

_____

PASSWORD

_____

SECURITY QUESTIONS

_____

NOTES

WEBSITE

_____

USERNAME

_____

PASSWORD

_____

SECURITY QUESTIONS

_____

NOTES

WEBSITE

_____

USERNAME

_____

PASSWORD

_____

SECURITY QUESTIONS

_____

NOTES

WEBSITE

_____

USERNAME

_____

PASSWORD

_____

SECURITY QUESTIONS

_____

NOTES

 # WTF is My Password?

WEBSITE

USERNAME

PASSWORD

SECURITY QUESTIONS

WEBSITE

USERNAME

PASSWORD

SECURITY QUESTIONS

WEBSITE

USERNAME

PASSWORD

SECURITY QUESTIONS

WEBSITE

USERNAME

PASSWORD

SECURITY QUESTIONS

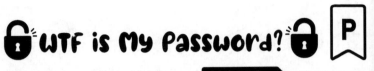

WTF is My Password?

P

WEBSITE
_____

USERNAME
_____

PASSWORD
_____

SECURITY QUESTIONS
_____

NOTES

WEBSITE
_____

USERNAME
_____

PASSWORD
_____

SECURITY QUESTIONS
_____

NOTES

WEBSITE
_____

USERNAME
_____

PASSWORD
_____

SECURITY QUESTIONS
_____

NOTES

WEBSITE
_____

USERNAME
_____

PASSWORD
_____

SECURITY QUESTIONS
_____

NOTES

 WTF is My Password?

WEBSITE

USERNAME

PASSWORD

SECURITY QUESTIONS

NOTES

WEBSITE

USERNAME

PASSWORD

SECURITY QUESTIONS

NOTES

WEBSITE

USERNAME

PASSWORD

SECURITY QUESTIONS

NOTES

WEBSITE

USERNAME

PASSWORD

SECURITY QUESTIONS

NOTES

WTF is My Password? P

WEBSITE

_____

USERNAME

_____

PASSWORD

_____

SECURITY QUESTIONS

_____

NOTES

WEBSITE

_____

USERNAME

_____

PASSWORD

_____

SECURITY QUESTIONS

_____

NOTES

WEBSITE

_____

USERNAME

_____

PASSWORD

_____

SECURITY QUESTIONS

_____

NOTES

WEBSITE

_____

USERNAME

_____

PASSWORD

_____

SECURITY QUESTIONS

_____

NOTES

WTF is My Password?

WEBSITE

USERNAME

PASSWORD

SECURITY QUESTIONS

NOTES

WEBSITE

USERNAME

PASSWORD

SECURITY QUESTIONS

NOTES

WEBSITE

USERNAME

PASSWORD

SECURITY QUESTIONS

NOTES

WEBSITE

USERNAME

PASSWORD

SECURITY QUESTIONS

NOTES

WTF is My Password?

WEBSITE
_____

USERNAME
_____

PASSWORD
_____

SECURITY QUESTIONS
_____

NOTES

WEBSITE
_____

USERNAME
_____

PASSWORD
_____

SECURITY QUESTIONS
_____

NOTES

WEBSITE
_____

USERNAME
_____

PASSWORD
_____

SECURITY QUESTIONS
_____

NOTES

WEBSITE
_____

USERNAME
_____

PASSWORD
_____

SECURITY QUESTIONS
_____

NOTES

WTF is My Password?

WEBSITE

USERNAME

PASSWORD

SECURITY QUESTIONS

NOTES

WEBSITE

USERNAME

PASSWORD

SECURITY QUESTIONS

NOTES

WEBSITE

USERNAME

PASSWORD

SECURITY QUESTIONS

NOTES

WEBSITE

USERNAME

PASSWORD

SECURITY QUESTIONS

NOTES

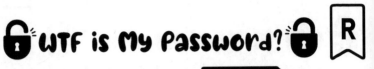

WTF is My Password?

WEBSITE
_____
USERNAME
_____
PASSWORD
_____
SECURITY QUESTIONS
_____

NOTES

WEBSITE
_____
USERNAME
_____
PASSWORD
_____
SECURITY QUESTIONS
_____

NOTES

WEBSITE
_____
USERNAME
_____
PASSWORD
_____
SECURITY QUESTIONS
_____

NOTES

WEBSITE
_____
USERNAME
_____
PASSWORD
_____
SECURITY QUESTIONS
_____

NOTES

 WTF is My Password?

WEBSITE

USERNAME

PASSWORD

SECURITY QUESTIONS

NOTES

WEBSITE

USERNAME

PASSWORD

SECURITY QUESTIONS

NOTES

WEBSITE

USERNAME

PASSWORD

SECURITY QUESTIONS

NOTES

WEBSITE

USERNAME

PASSWORD

SECURITY QUESTIONS

NOTES

WTF is My Password?

R

WEBSITE
_____

USERNAME
_____

PASSWORD
_____

SECURITY QUESTIONS
_____

NOTES

WEBSITE
_____

USERNAME
_____

PASSWORD
_____

SECURITY QUESTIONS
_____

NOTES

WEBSITE
_____

USERNAME
_____

PASSWORD
_____

SECURITY QUESTIONS
_____

NOTES

WEBSITE
_____

USERNAME
_____

PASSWORD
_____

SECURITY QUESTIONS
_____

NOTES

 WTF is My Password? S

WEBSITE

_____

USERNAME

_____

PASSWORD

_____

SECURITY QUESTIONS

_____

 NOTES

WEBSITE

_____

USERNAME

_____

PASSWORD

_____

SECURITY QUESTIONS

_____

NOTES

WEBSITE

_____

USERNAME

_____

PASSWORD

_____

SECURITY QUESTIONS

_____

NOTES

WEBSITE

_____

USERNAME

_____

PASSWORD

_____

SECURITY QUESTIONS

_____

 NOTES

WTF is My Password?

S

WEBSITE
_____

USERNAME
_____

PASSWORD
_____

SECURITY QUESTIONS
_____

NOTES

WEBSITE
_____

USERNAME
_____

PASSWORD
_____

SECURITY QUESTIONS
_____

NOTES

WEBSITE
_____

USERNAME
_____

PASSWORD
_____

SECURITY QUESTIONS
_____

NOTES

WEBSITE
_____

USERNAME
_____

PASSWORD
_____

SECURITY QUESTIONS
_____

NOTES

WTF is My Password? S

WEBSITE
_____

USERNAME
_____

PASSWORD
_____

SECURITY QUESTIONS
_____

NOTES

WEBSITE
_____

USERNAME
_____

PASSWORD
_____

SECURITY QUESTIONS
_____

NOTES

WEBSITE
_____

USERNAME
_____

PASSWORD
_____

SECURITY QUESTIONS
_____

NOTES

WEBSITE
_____

USERNAME
_____

PASSWORD
_____

SECURITY QUESTIONS
_____

NOTES

WTF is My Password?

WEBSITE

USERNAME

PASSWORD

SECURITY QUESTIONS

NOTES

WEBSITE

USERNAME

PASSWORD

SECURITY QUESTIONS

NOTES

WEBSITE

USERNAME

PASSWORD

SECURITY QUESTIONS

NOTES

WEBSITE

USERNAME

PASSWORD

SECURITY QUESTIONS

NOTES

WTF is My Password?

WEBSITE

USERNAME

PASSWORD

SECURITY QUESTIONS

NOTES

WEBSITE

USERNAME

PASSWORD

SECURITY QUESTIONS

NOTES

WEBSITE

USERNAME

PASSWORD

SECURITY QUESTIONS

NOTES

WEBSITE

USERNAME

PASSWORD

SECURITY QUESTIONS

NOTES

WTF is My Password?

WEBSITE

USERNAME

PASSWORD

SECURITY QUESTIONS

NOTES

WEBSITE

USERNAME

PASSWORD

SECURITY QUESTIONS

NOTES

WEBSITE

USERNAME

PASSWORD

SECURITY QUESTIONS

NOTES

WEBSITE

USERNAME

PASSWORD

SECURITY QUESTIONS

NOTES

 WTF is My Password?

WEBSITE

USERNAME

PASSWORD

SECURITY QUESTIONS

NOTES

WEBSITE

USERNAME

PASSWORD

SECURITY QUESTIONS

NOTES

WEBSITE

USERNAME

PASSWORD

SECURITY QUESTIONS

NOTES

WEBSITE

USERNAME

PASSWORD

SECURITY QUESTIONS

NOTES

WTF is My Password?

WEBSITE
_____

USERNAME
_____

PASSWORD
_____

SECURITY QUESTIONS
_____

NOTES

WEBSITE
_____

USERNAME
_____

PASSWORD
_____

SECURITY QUESTIONS
_____

NOTES

WEBSITE
_____

USERNAME
_____

PASSWORD
_____

SECURITY QUESTIONS
_____

NOTES

WEBSITE
_____

USERNAME
_____

PASSWORD
_____

SECURITY QUESTIONS
_____

NOTES

WTF is My Password?

WEBSITE
_____
USERNAME
_____
PASSWORD
_____
SECURITY QUESTIONS
_____

NOTES

WEBSITE
_____
USERNAME
_____
PASSWORD
_____
SECURITY QUESTIONS
_____

NOTES

WEBSITE
_____
USERNAME
_____
PASSWORD
_____
SECURITY QUESTIONS
_____

NOTES

WEBSITE
_____
USERNAME
_____
PASSWORD
_____
SECURITY QUESTIONS
_____

NOTES

 # WTF is My Password?

WEBSITE
_____

USERNAME
_____

PASSWORD
_____

SECURITY QUESTIONS
_____

NOTES

WEBSITE
_____

USERNAME
_____

PASSWORD
_____

SECURITY QUESTIONS
_____

NOTES

WEBSITE
_____

USERNAME
_____

PASSWORD
_____

SECURITY QUESTIONS
_____

NOTES

WEBSITE
_____

USERNAME
_____

PASSWORD
_____

SECURITY QUESTIONS
_____

NOTES

WTF is My Password?

WEBSITE

USERNAME

PASSWORD

SECURITY QUESTIONS

NOTES

WEBSITE

USERNAME

PASSWORD

SECURITY QUESTIONS

NOTES

WEBSITE

USERNAME

PASSWORD

SECURITY QUESTIONS

NOTES

WEBSITE

USERNAME

PASSWORD

SECURITY QUESTIONS

NOTES

WTF is My Password? V

WEBSITE
_____

USERNAME
_____

PASSWORD
_____

SECURITY QUESTIONS
_____

NOTES

WEBSITE
_____

USERNAME
_____

PASSWORD
_____

SECURITY QUESTIONS
_____

NOTES

WEBSITE
_____

USERNAME
_____

PASSWORD
_____

SECURITY QUESTIONS
_____

NOTES

WEBSITE
_____

USERNAME
_____

PASSWORD
_____

SECURITY QUESTIONS
_____

NOTES

 # WTF is My Password?

WEBSITE

_____

USERNAME

_____

PASSWORD

_____

SECURITY QUESTIONS

_____

NOTES

WEBSITE

_____

USERNAME

_____

PASSWORD

_____

SECURITY QUESTIONS

_____

NOTES

WEBSITE

_____

USERNAME

_____

PASSWORD

_____

SECURITY QUESTIONS

_____

NOTES

WEBSITE

_____

USERNAME

_____

PASSWORD

_____

SECURITY QUESTIONS

_____

NOTES

WTF is My Password?

WEBSITE

_____

USERNAME

_____

PASSWORD

_____

SECURITY QUESTIONS

_____

NOTES

WEBSITE

_____

USERNAME

_____

PASSWORD

_____

SECURITY QUESTIONS

_____

NOTES

WEBSITE

_____

USERNAME

_____

PASSWORD

_____

SECURITY QUESTIONS

_____

NOTES

WEBSITE

_____

USERNAME

_____

PASSWORD

_____

SECURITY QUESTIONS

_____

NOTES

 # WTF is My Password?

WEBSITE

_____

USERNAME

_____

PASSWORD

_____

SECURITY QUESTIONS

_____

NOTES

WEBSITE

_____

USERNAME

_____

PASSWORD

_____

SECURITY QUESTIONS

_____

NOTES

WEBSITE

_____

USERNAME

_____

PASSWORD

_____

SECURITY QUESTIONS

_____

NOTES

WEBSITE

_____

USERNAME

_____

PASSWORD

_____

SECURITY QUESTIONS

_____

NOTES

🔓 WTF is My Password? 🔒 [X]

WEBSITE
_____
USERNAME
_____
PASSWORD
_____
SECURITY QUESTIONS
_____

NOTES

WEBSITE
_____
USERNAME
_____
PASSWORD
_____
SECURITY QUESTIONS
_____

NOTES

WEBSITE
_____
USERNAME
_____
PASSWORD
_____
SECURITY QUESTIONS
_____

NOTES

WEBSITE
_____
USERNAME
_____
PASSWORD
_____
SECURITY QUESTIONS
_____

NOTES

 WTF is My Password?

WEBSITE

USERNAME

PASSWORD

SECURITY QUESTIONS

NOTES

WEBSITE

USERNAME

PASSWORD

SECURITY QUESTIONS

NOTES

WEBSITE

USERNAME

PASSWORD

SECURITY QUESTIONS

NOTES

WEBSITE

USERNAME

PASSWORD

SECURITY QUESTIONS

NOTES

 # WTF is My Password?

WEBSITE

_____

USERNAME

_____

PASSWORD

_____

SECURITY QUESTIONS

_____

NOTES

WEBSITE

_____

USERNAME

_____

PASSWORD

_____

SECURITY QUESTIONS

_____

NOTES

WEBSITE

_____

USERNAME

_____

PASSWORD

_____

SECURITY QUESTIONS

_____

NOTES

WEBSITE

_____

USERNAME

_____

PASSWORD

_____

SECURITY QUESTIONS

_____

NOTES

 WTF is My Password?

WEBSITE
_____
USERNAME
_____
PASSWORD
_____
SECURITY QUESTIONS
_____

NOTES

WEBSITE
_____
USERNAME
_____
PASSWORD
_____
SECURITY QUESTIONS
_____

NOTES

WEBSITE
_____
USERNAME
_____
PASSWORD
_____
SECURITY QUESTIONS
_____

NOTES

WEBSITE
_____
USERNAME
_____
PASSWORD
_____
SECURITY QUESTIONS
_____

NOTES

WTF is My Password?

WEBSITE

USERNAME

PASSWORD

SECURITY QUESTIONS

NOTES

WEBSITE

USERNAME

PASSWORD

SECURITY QUESTIONS

NOTES

WEBSITE

USERNAME

PASSWORD

SECURITY QUESTIONS

NOTES

WEBSITE

USERNAME

PASSWORD

SECURITY QUESTIONS

NOTES

 # WTF is My Password?

WEBSITE
_____

USERNAME
_____

PASSWORD
_____

SECURITY QUESTIONS
_____

NOTES

WEBSITE
_____

USERNAME
_____

PASSWORD
_____

SECURITY QUESTIONS
_____

NOTES

WEBSITE
_____

USERNAME
_____

PASSWORD
_____

SECURITY QUESTIONS
_____

NOTES

WEBSITE
_____

USERNAME
_____

PASSWORD
_____

SECURITY QUESTIONS
_____

NOTES

🔓 WTF is My Password? 🔓 [Z]

WEBSITE
_____

USERNAME
_____

PASSWORD
_____

SECURITY QUESTIONS
_____

NOTES

WEBSITE
_____

USERNAME
_____

PASSWORD
_____

SECURITY QUESTIONS
_____

NOTES

WEBSITE
_____

USERNAME
_____

PASSWORD
_____

SECURITY QUESTIONS
_____

NOTES

WEBSITE
_____

USERNAME
_____

PASSWORD
_____

SECURITY QUESTIONS
_____

NOTES

WTF is My Password?

Z

WEBSITE

USERNAME

PASSWORD

SECURITY QUESTIONS

NOTES

WEBSITE

USERNAME

PASSWORD

SECURITY QUESTIONS

NOTES

WEBSITE

USERNAME

PASSWORD

SECURITY QUESTIONS

NOTES

WEBSITE

USERNAME

PASSWORD

SECURITY QUESTIONS

NOTES

WTF is My Password? Z

WEBSITE

USERNAME

PASSWORD

SECURITY QUESTIONS

NOTES

WEBSITE

USERNAME

PASSWORD

SECURITY QUESTIONS

NOTES

WEBSITE

USERNAME

PASSWORD

SECURITY QUESTIONS

NOTES

WEBSITE

USERNAME

PASSWORD

SECURITY QUESTIONS

NOTES

JUST WRITE
THE DAMN THING!

Just Write The Damn Thing!

_____

_____

_____

_____

_____

_____

_____

_____

_____

_____

_____

_____

_____

_____

_____

_____

_____

_____

_____

_____

JUST WRITE
THE DAMN THING!

Just Write
The Damn Thing!

JUST WRITE
THE DAMN THING!

Just Write The Damn Thing!

Made in the USA
Columbia, SC
15 December 2024

49391174R00050